RESCUED RIVERS

PATHFINDER EDITION

By Greta Gilbert

Contents

Winding Their Way

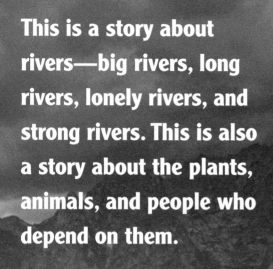

This is a story about rivers—big rivers, long rivers, lonely rivers, and strong rivers. This is also a story about the plants, animals, and people who depend on them.

CHANCES ARE, you are one of those people. That's because in the United States, 80 percent of the water people use comes from lakes and rivers. Rivers help water crops, cool machines, and even create energy. That means when you wash your hands, eat a peach, or simply turn on the lights, it may be thanks to a river.

The United States is lucky. Many large rivers flow through the country, and fresh water is relatively abundant, or plentiful. There is a problem, however. The fresh water isn't evenly distributed. In some parts of the country, there is a lot of it, and floods are common. In other regions, there is often not enough fresh water to meet people's needs.

Throughout history, people in the United States have modified, or changed, rivers to help solve this problem of availability and distribution. Some of the changes people have made to rivers are amazing. Others are downright shocking. Read on to discover some of the twists and turns in the winding story of U.S. rivers.

By Greta Gilbert

Big River

MISSISSIPPI

Writer Mark Twain once wrote, "The Mississippi will always have its own way; no engineering skill can persuade it to do otherwise." He lived in the 1800s, a time when North America's largest river, the Mississippi, was considered wild and unpredictable. Why? In a word: floods.

The floods of the Mississippi are legendary. Water once poured over the forests around the river for hundreds of miles. "It was a most magnificent spectacle to behold," wrote one early explorer. "Nothing was visible except the pine needles and branches of the highest trees."

The floods watered the land, and they also nourished it. Floating in the floodwaters were tiny bits of dirt and decomposed materials. These materials, called **sediments**, fed plants and tiny animals. The tiny animals grew and fed bigger animals—deer, wild turkeys, bison, and even alligators. All this natural abundance soon brought farmers, too.

Many farmers settled in the **floodplains** of the Mississippi and its **tributaries**. They couldn't believe their luck. The soils were very rich, and crops grew easily.

Farmers cut down the forests that surrounded the river. They drained **wetlands** to make room for more farms. What did they do about the floods? They built **levees**, or long mounds of dirt that ran beside the river.

The levees helped control the floods—usually. But with more people and fewer wetlands to help absorb floodwaters, over the years floods grew more damaging. Then, in 1993, a massive flood hit the Mississippi. It swallowed whole towns and did more damage than any flood in U.S. history.

The Mississippi Flood of 1993 surprised many people. It made them consider how they could have decreased its impact.

Today, people are working hard to restore natural wetlands in and around the Mississippi. They know that by doing so, they are not only helping themselves; they are also helping all the living things that depend on the river.

In 1993, the Mississippi River washed over its levees and flooded the la...

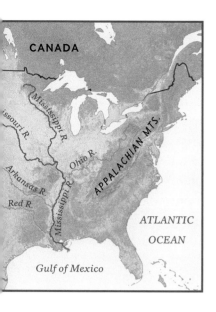

Dams like this one on the Missouri River protect people from floods.

Long River
MISSOURI

As people settled the western United States, many of them followed the path of Lewis and Clark. That path led along the winding route of America's longest river, the Missouri.

Like the Mississippi, the Missouri is a moody, unpredictable river. During its spring floods, the river cuts into its own soft banks, causing them to collapse. The naturally muddy water that results has earned the river the nickname "Muddy Mo."

The "mud" in the Missouri's water is really sediment. The plants and animals of the river's ecosystem need it to survive. One of those animals, the paddlefish, is a giant river fish with a mouth like a bucket and a nose like a beaver's tail.

Also known as the "spoonbill catfish," the paddlefish has receptors on the bottom of its snout. They help it sense tiny animals that live in the murky river water. With its giant mouth open, it scoops up these animals for food. Over time, an adult paddlefish can grow more than six feet long and weigh more than 200 pounds. That's one big fish!

Today's paddlefish population is only 10 to 20 percent of what it was when Lewis and Clark paddled up the Missouri. Why? One reason is dams. Over the years, many large dams have been built along the Missouri. Like levees, these dams help people. They control floods and store water for people to use. However, the dams also decrease paddlefish habitat. They cause river water to flow quickly. This washes away the calm, muddy water where paddlefish feed.

Luckily, people are working to save the paddlefish and the river habitat it depends on. Breeding areas have been protected on the Upper Missouri and Yellowstone Rivers, and riverside habitat is being restored. Changes like these help ensure a future for this wide-mouthed ambassador of some of America's largest rivers, including the Missouri.

Paddlefish

Lonely River
COLORADO

Some people moving west chose to follow a southwestern route. That route took them through the driest, most inhospitable part of the United States, the Desert Southwest.

In 1869, the western explorer John Wesley Powell and his crew found themselves in the heart of this rugged region. They were stuck in the deepest, most isolated canyon they had ever seen. Their only way out was a river with rapids as big as three-story houses.

That canyon was the Grand Canyon, and the river was the Colorado. Back then, the Colorado ran wild and uninterrupted to the sea. Together with its tributaries, it was a lonely lifeline for the region, known as the Plateau Province. It included parts of Colorado, Utah, Arizona, New Mexico, and Nevada.

Powell's trip confirmed what many settlers had feared. Any farmer wishing to make a living in this area would need a lot of land and a lot of water. Even then, crops would be few, and life would be difficult.

If Powell revisited the Desert Southwest today, he would be amazed. Where there once was a dusty desert, green fields bloom. Where once there were fields of cacti, cities buzz. And along most of the Colorado River, there are **reservoirs** instead of rapids.

Thanks to dams along the Colorado River and its tributaries, America's most hostile terrain is now some of its most productive. However, there is still not enough water to meet everyone's needs. In some years, for example, people draw so much water from the Colorado that it stops flowing before it reaches the sea.

The good news is that people living in the Desert Southwest are working hard to live within the limits of the Colorado. By conserving its water, they are respecting their lonely lifeline and protecting it.

The Glen Canyon Dam on the Colorado River creates Lake Powell.

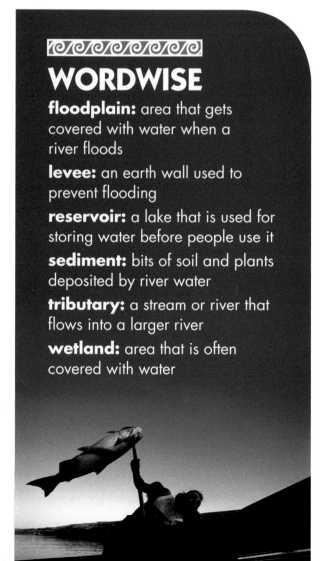

The Columbia River rushes through a spillway at the Bonneville Dam.

WORDWISE

floodplain: area that gets covered with water when a river floods

levee: an earth wall used to prevent flooding

reservoir: a lake that is used for storing water before people use it

sediment: bits of soil and plants deposited by river water

tributary: a stream or river that flows into a larger river

wetland: area that is often covered with water

Strong River
COLUMBIA

Dams not only store water for people and help control floods. They can also create energy. President Franklin Roosevelt knew this. When he visited the Columbia River, he said it was terrible to see so much water running down to the sea. He wanted to use that water to make energy instead.

No wonder. The Columbia is America's most powerful river. It whooshes down from the Canadian Rocky Mountains with incredible force. Compared to other rivers, the Columbia River is very steep, and that steepness gives it a lot of power.

That power is not a problem for a tough, tireless fish called the salmon. Born in the gravel of cold mountain streams, the Columbia salmon migrates thousands of miles to the ocean. Then, at the end of its life, it journeys back up the Columbia to its birth stream to spawn, or reproduce.

Swimming up the Columbia to spawn can't be easy. In the past, the river's flow surged at 1,240,000 cubic feet per second. That's an incredible amount of energy! The Columbia River's Grand Coulee Dam was completed in 1942 to capture that energy. The dam generates enough power every year to supply 2.3 million households with electricity.

The dam was good news for people but bad news for salmon. They simply couldn't get past the dam to spawn. Today, the number of salmon in the Columbia is 3 percent of what it was before the Grand Coulee Dam was built.

People are working hard to solve this problem. Fish ladders have been installed to help returning salmon move past many dams along the Columbia and its tributaries. In addition, scheduled "spilling" over the dams in the spring helps young salmon on their way down the river to the sea.

A Yakima man fishes for salmon on the Columbia River.

Rivers Transformed

Levees and dams aren't the only ways people change rivers. In California, for example, rivers have been completely transformed.

Why? The reason is simple. Most of the water in California is in the northern part of the state, while most of the people and farms are in the southern part.

To solve this problem, Californians rely on two mighty rivers—the Sacramento and the San Joaquin. Through a complex system of pumps and pipes, much of their water is drained off in the middle of the state. From there, the rivers begin their journey southward along artificial rivers such as the California Aqueduct.

These concrete river highways provide water to more than 25 million people from San Francisco to San Diego, for drinking, washing, and watering plants and animals. They also allow millions of acres of farmland to grow, which in turn lets California farmers produce half of the country's fruits, nuts, and vegetables.

Still, there is not enough water for the people of California, and they continue to search for new ways to get water, as well as ways to conserve the water they have.

The California Aqueduct carries water to the southern part of the state.

The delta's water comes from the Sacramento and San Joaquin Rivers.

1 Steele's Mill Dam is at the center of this historic photo.

2 Steele's Mill Dam is removed.

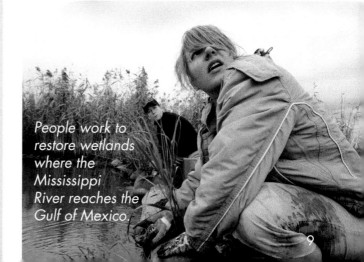

People work to restore wetlands where the Mississippi River reaches the Gulf of Mexico.

The Story Winds On

Today, people are learning more about the importance of river ecosystems. They are also beginning to accept that modifying, or changing, rivers can't solve all their water distribution problems.

One way people are working to protect rivers is by trying to use less water. In Las Vegas, Nevada, for example, people receive money if they replace their thirsty lawns with native, water-conserving plants. In many other cities, people are rewarded for installing low-flow toilets and showerheads in their homes.

In addition, farmers are installing more efficient underground "drip" watering systems and planting crops that need less water.

Finally, wetlands across America are being restored. In Florida, for example, engineers are working to restore the Kissimmee River. It flows down from the middle of the state and feeds the Everglades—one of the most important wildlife habitats in the United States.

In New York and California, people have decided to spend money to restore wetlands rather than adding more water treatment plants. They have realized that the wetlands will do the job just as well, naturally.

All across the United States, kids are learning about rivers, too. Thousands of kids participate in "Adopt-a-River" programs and river clean ups throughout the country. You see, the story of U.S. rivers is not over. You get to write the next chapter. That's good news for this country. And it's good news for rivers.

3 Steele's Mill Dam is gone, and Hitchcock Creek runs freely today.

Restoring RIVERS

This fish ladder allows salmon to move past the Bonneville Dam as they swim upstream to spawn.

Columbia River

WA

OR

NV

CA

AZ

Colorado River

NM

Rio Grande River

TX

People and businesses around Las Vegas are replacing grass with native desert plants. They get money as a reward. They also save Colorado River water.

Numerous groups are working along the Rio Grande to restore wetlands and riverside woodlands, called bosques. These projects provide important habitat for native fish species and wintering birds, including the sandhill crane.

People all around the United States are helping to restore rivers. Take a look at some of the projects they're working on.

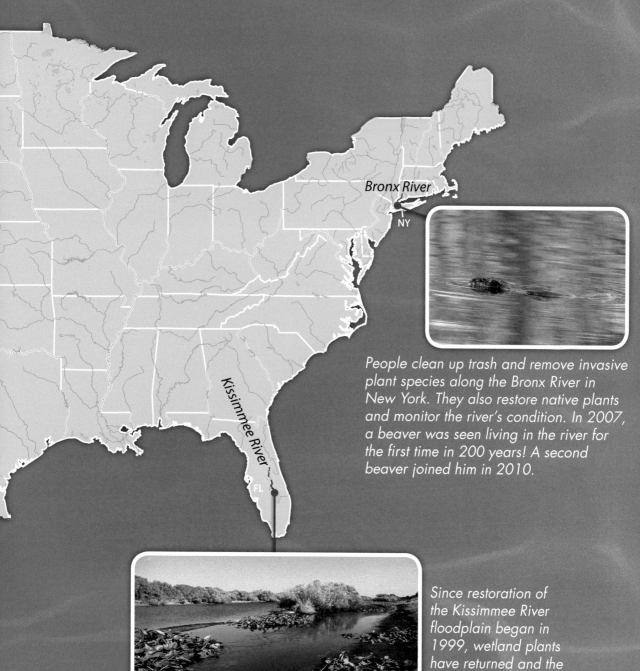

Bronx River

NY

People clean up trash and remove invasive plant species along the Bronx River in New York. They also restore native plants and monitor the river's condition. In 2007, a beaver was seen living in the river for the first time in 200 years! A second beaver joined him in 2010.

Kissimmee River

FL

Since restoration of the Kissimmee River floodplain began in 1999, wetland plants have returned and the numbers of wading birds and waterfowl have increased.

Water for Life

Answer these questions to help keep rivers flowing!

1 How do floods on the Mississippi River bring both benefits and disadvantages?

2 How do dams on the Missouri River affect paddlefish habitat?

3 Why doesn't the Colorado River flow all the way to the sea in some years?

4 What are the most important ideas about salmon in the article?

5 How are river restoration projects helping to protect the plants and animals that depend on river habitats?